TO

WITH LOVE

Book of of Manners

for Boys

Precious Moments® Book of Manners for Boys
Text by Janna Walkup
Published by Harvest House Publishers
Eugene, Oregon 97402

Precious Moments® Book of Manners for Boys
Text copyright © 2006 by Harvest House Publishers, Inc.
Eugene, OR 97402

ISBN-13: 978-0-7369-1526-7
ISBN-10: 0-7369-1526-5

Design and production by Koechel Peterson & Associates, Inc.
Minneapolis, MN

Printed in Hong Kong

06 07 08 09 10 11 12 13 / NG / 10 9 8 7 6 5 4 3 2 1

CONTENTS

Manners Matter!

Do you like giving your family great big hugs and high-fives? Is playing kickball or baseball with your pals one of your favorite things to do? Does helping your dad build a fort out of branches, blankets, and boards sound like a great way to spend an afternoon?

If you like to have fun and play with your family and friends, you'll have a great time learning about and practicing good manners!

Manners are the things we say and the way we live and play that help us show other people that we love and care about them. Everything you do—eating your lunch, building block towers with your best friend, opening presents during the holidays—is more fun for everyone when you use your best manners.

It's fun to practice using good manners with your family and your friends. You can even play good manners games with your plastic animals and play figures! You can practice being friendly and fair. You can practice using polite words and speaking clearly. You can practice taking turns and letting others go first.

Good people have good manners. Good manners let other people know that they are important to you. Good manners say, "I love you!"

My Talking Manners
SAYING HELLO, SAYING GOODBYE

Just a few years ago you were probably saying your very first words—*mama* or *car* or *doggie* or *duck*. Now you know the right words for just about everything! That means you're ready to learn the right words to say at the right times.

Meeting and Greeting

The first thing to know about good talking manners is how to say hello. When someone walks into a room, it's polite to stand up to greet them. Smile big and look right at the person with your grinning face.

If you've never met the person before, or if the person is a grown-up you don't know very well, it's good manners to shake hands with them. Shaking hands is another way to say, "I'm happy to meet you." If the person is already a good friend or a favorite relative, you can greet them in a special way—a fancy handshake or a fun high-five or a big hug. Just do whatever feels comfortable to you!

When you're talking to someone, always say your words clearly and try to put a friendly look on your face. If someone says something to you that doesn't make sense, you can just say, "Excuse me?" or "Pardon me?" or "Could you please repeat that?" The other person will be happy to say it again.

The Name Game

People really like it when you use their name. It makes them feel good. So say, "Hello, Uncle Ron!" Or, "It's great to see you, Jacob!" You can even use a pet's name: "How's it going, Lightning?"

Instead of saying, "Hey," always say, "Hello!" or just a nice, friendly, "Hi!"

If you don't know someone's name, go ahead and tell them your own name. Then you can say, "What is your name?" They will be happy to tell you.

When you meet a grown-up, always call them by Mrs., Miss, or Mr. and their last name—Mrs. Smith, Mr. Watermelon, Miss Seaturtle—unless they ask you to please call them something else. And even if they want you to call them by their first name, it's a little more respectful to use a title with their name. You can call your soccer coach Mr. Mike or your music teacher Miss Melody. It shows that you look up to them and that you are willing to listen to and learn from them. And sometimes grown-ups will return the favor and say "Mister" along with your name. That makes you feel really important—and like a very big guy!

Everyone Plays!

When you are with a group of kids—in a classroom, on the field with a team, at the park—it's very important that you are kind to everyone in the group. Try to talk to all of the kids if you can. Never, ever say something mean or unkind to or about someone—even if you're only just joking around. You might not intend to hurt someone's feelings, but nobody wants to be on the receiving end of put-downs or rude jokes.

If you wonder if one of your jokes might make someone feel bad, it's better not to say anything at all. What you can do is get to know everyone and include them in your play. That way everyone feels a part of things—and everyone feels important!

Learning to Listen

When someone is talking, be sure to let them finish what they're saying before you start to talk. It might sound kind of silly, but part of talking is listening. And good listeners make good friends!

If two people are talking and you really need to say something, just use your politest words to let them know that you have something very important to say: "May I speak to you?" "May I please tell you something?" And only do this if you *really* need to talk to them—if your dad's truck is rolling down the driveway, for instance!

Until Next Time!

The final part of talking manners happens when you're ready to go. You say goodbye!

But you don't just say, "See ya!" or "Later!" and run off to play. You go up to the person you are saying goodbye to and tell them that you had a good time: "Goodbye! It was great playing with you!" Then you can say goodbye in your own special way—a high-five, a crazy handshake, a silly face.

My Kindness
Manners
SAYING WHAT IS NICE

Did you know that certain words are "magic" words? Now, these words don't work exactly like a magic spell or a magic trick. You can't shout, "Abracadabra!" and find your chores magically done—the dog fed, your room cleaned, the recycling sorted. But these words do put everyone around you in a good mood. And when you use these magic words, they put *you* in a good mood, too!

Please. Thank you. Excuse me. I'm sorry.

You can use them when you need something. You can use these "magic" words when someone has done something nice for you. You can use them when you said or did something that you wish you hadn't said or done. "Magic" words are like Band-Aids that make everything all better!

Super Nice Words

Speak kindly to everyone, but remember to use super nice words with the people you see every day—your mom and dad, your brother and sister, your teacher or coach, your best friend down the street.

Also, use words that are honest and true. You shouldn't say things that aren't true (unless you're just being silly and making up a funny story, of course!) because that could make someone feel bad. It also might make them not want to hang around with you. Super nice words make everyone glad!

Thanks a Bunch!

"Thank you!" Say these words when people do nice things for you—when your uncle takes you out for a double-decker ice cream cone, when your mom buys you a new book or game, when your sister helps you clean your room.

When you say "thank you," it makes other people want to do nice things for you. And you'll want to do nice things for them. And pretty soon everyone will be doing nice things for everyone else! Thank-you manners make the world a very good place!

A Letter Is Even Better

Do you know what is even better than *saying* thank you? Giving someone a thank-you note! Even if you don't know how to write yet, a thank-you picture is just as good (maybe even better!).

Say "Please"!

If you need something, always add the words "please" or "may I?" to your request. Saying "please"—and then saying "thank you" when you are given what you asked for—are sure ways to get what you need.

I'm Very Sorry

When something goes wrong and you've made someone feel sad or broken something, you might want to get really angry or upset. It's all right to use words that let others know how you feel ("I feel so frustrated!" or "That makes me so mad when that happens!"). When you're feeling a little bit calmer, you can just say, "I'm sorry" or "Please excuse me." Then the other person will say, "I forgive you." Doing something fun together—playing a game, reading a story—can make things happy again.

My Friendship Manners
GETTING ALONG WITH PALS

One of the best things about getting bigger and growing up is making new friends. You can play and hang out with so many fun people! You can meet them at the park, in your neighborhood, at school, at church, on a team—anywhere you go, you're sure to find some terrific pals.

The Key to Getting Along

Have you ever heard of the Golden Rule? It's a short, easy-to-remember saying that tells you all you need to know about getting along with other people:

Do unto others as you would have them do unto you.

The key to getting along with pals is doing good things for each other.

Good friends always stick together and are there for each other.

Good friends always say nice things to and help each other.

Good friends always listen to each other.

Good friends always have a great time playing together.

Fun and Games

When you're playing games with your friends, make sure you always follow the rules and tell the truth. Use good words and don't make a big deal if you win or lose. What matters is that you try your best, encourage and support each other ("Nice job!" "Great shot!"), and have a ton of fun.

Sometimes playtime can get kind of wild. It's fun to run around with your friends, playing chase and tag, having races and acting crazy. But you should never throw things (like sand, sticks, or rocks) at people, call someone a name, or make mean faces. These things can hurt people on the outside and on the inside. Remember that Golden Rule! Only do something to someone if you would want the very same thing done to you.

Share Your Stuff

Good friends use the best kind of sharing manners with each other. Sharing is a way of saying, "You're cool. I like being friends with you. Let's do stuff together!"

If you have a whole bunch of plastic snakes or a drawer full of activity books, it's nice to give some to your friend. You should check with a parent first, but your mom or dad will probably say that it's fine to give away some of your things—especially if your friend doesn't have as much as you have.

Way to Play!

Sharing happens all the time when you play with your pals—even if you aren't playing indoors with Legos or toy cars! For instance, sometimes it takes friends a little while to figure out what game to play. You want to dig a tunnel in the dirt, but your friend wants to ride scooters. What should you do?

It's not very fun to stand around and argue about it. It is fun to play. So share your imaginative ideas. Play your friend's game first. Say, "Let's ride scooters until snack time. And then after we eat our snack, we can dig tunnels."

"Hey, can you come over to play?" Everyone likes to hear those words! It's fun to invite friends over to your house. And it's just as great to spend the afternoon hanging out at their house! Good manners can make playtime lots of fun for everyone. So what are we waiting for? Let's play!

Welcome to My House!

Here's a giant word: *hospitality*. It sounds like a grown-up word, but it's actually kids who have the chance to show hospitality the most. After all, who plays with their pals more—you or your parents? You probably do!

Hospitality sounds like something hard, but it's really pretty easy. Showing hospitality just means that when friends come over to your house, your job is to help them feel welcome and relaxed.

Friends First

When you're using your playing manners, here's one super important rule to remember: Your guest (the friend who's over at your house) always goes first. Let him have the first choice of fruit leather or popsicle flavor. When you play a game, he gets the first turn. If there's just one crazy straw left, he gets it.

Come On In!

When your friend comes over to play, the first thing you should do is meet him at the door and say, "Hi, I'm glad you're here. Come on in!"

Then you can show him where to put his coat, tell him if he needs to take off his shoes or if he can leave them on, and let him know where he can put anything else he brought.

It's always helpful to let your friend know where the bathroom is. You can let him know about any important rules you have in your house: "We can climb on the rock wall in the basement, but we can't swing from the chandelier in the dining room."

My Favorite Things

Playing with friends in your room or playroom is really fun. But what happens when you both want to play with the exact same toy? Remember the rule about letting your friend have the first choice. If he wants to wear your superhero cape, you should let him. You can always wear it after your friend goes home.

If you have some favorite things that are very important to you—and you don't want anyone else to play with them— you can ask your mom or dad to help you put these things away before your friend comes over.

Happy to Be Here

When you're a guest, the number-one thing to remember is that it should be easy for your friend's family to have you around. Just be kind and helpful and remember your "magic" manners words, and you'll do just fine.

Before you go in the house, wipe your feet at the door. Then you can walk in and say, "Thanks for having me over to play!" Inside the house, make sure you keep your feet off the furniture (no climbing—save that for trees and playground equipment!) and always ask before you pick up anything that looks important or breakable.

Sometimes you might work together on a big project—making a papier mache volcano or building a big ship out of chairs and blankets and clothes—that is a lot of fun but makes a big mess. Instead of letting your friend and his family clean up the mess, always help clean it up before you go home.

Follow the Rules

It's really important to remember that in your friend's house, they might follow different rules. Some rules are the same everywhere you go—for example, you should always, always wash your hands after going to the bathroom or before you eat something. But some things are done differently in different homes. Maybe your family eats burritos with their hands, but your friend's family eats them with a knife and fork.

The last thing to do comes at the very end of your visit. Always be sure to say a great big "thank you" to your friend and his family for having you over: "Thanks for inviting me over. I had a super fun time. Let's play again!"

My Helping Manners

DOING THINGS FOR MYSELF AND OTHERS

Everyone likes a helping hand! Helping is a way of saying, "Here, let me do something for you. I like you!" Or, "Let's do this together. The faster we finish it, the sooner we can play!"

Helping at Home
Have you ever noticed that sometimes your house is really clean—maybe when family friends are coming over for dinner, or when you're getting ready for the holidays—but other times it looks like it was just hit by a tornado?

You can do your part to help your family keep the house clean. It starts with you picking up after yourself. Put your toys back on the shelves. Keep all of your balls together in a basket. Put away your shirts and pants, and put your dirty socks in the laundry hamper.

When you're doing your chores, it's fun to turn them into a game. See how quickly you can vacuum the floor (but be sure it gets clean!). Pretend you're in a gold-medal race when you're sorting through the recycling. Pretend your dresser drawers are hungry dinosaur mouths and "feed" them your clean, folded clothes.

How Can I Help?

It's also good manners to help other people, even (or especially!) when you're not asked to. If your brother's job is to sweep the floor, hold the dustpan for him. If your teacher is handing out snacks to the class, ask, "May I help do that?"

It's always good manners to help your friends and your little brothers or little sisters. Your neighbors and older people—like grandparents—also love it when you say, "Is there anything I can do to help?"

Help Yourself

Did you know that you can also do some things to help yourself? As soon as you are able to, wash your face and brush your teeth. (You can have a parent help you finish up your teeth, but you can get them started.) After you get dressed in the morning, you can put away your pajamas very neatly. Learn how to tie your shoes, comb your hair, and do buttons and snaps. The more you do for yourself, the less your mom or dad has to do for you. And the more time you both have to make paper airplanes or play with your train set!

29

My Obeying Manners

DOING THE RIGHT THING AT THE RIGHT TIME

THIS WAY

NO THIS WAY

OVER HERE

THERE

ON MY WAY

"Yes, I will!"

"Okay, that sounds great!"

"No problem!"

These words are so awesome to hear. When you use your obeying manners, you show respect—or caring and love—to your parents and other grown-ups who help you—grandparents, teachers, and pastors.

Keeping Safe

Obeying keeps you safe. When you're in the car, you need to be buckled into your car seat in case the driver has to stop suddenly. When you're crossing the street, look both ways and hold hands with the adult you're with in case cars are going too fast. When you're playing ball outside, always ask a grown-up to get a ball that rolls into the street.

If you use your best obeying manners, you'll probably be able to start doing some things sooner. Maybe your dad will let you use some of the tools in his shop. Or your grandpa will let you play with his old train set. Or your big sister will let you help take care of her brand-new puppy.

Do It Right Away

When your mom or your teacher asks you to please do something, be sure to do it right away—with a great big grin. "I will" sounds much better than "I won't." And if they ask you to stop doing something, be sure to stop doing it right away, too!

If your parents tell you that you can't do something or have something—for example, you can't get out your new science experiment kit right before bedtime, or you can't wear shorts and a T-shirt in the pouring-down rain—it's best to just accept what they say and go on with the next thing. Pick out your favorite bedtime story. Have fun wearing your raincoat and boots and stomping in the puddles. Be sure not to keep pestering your parents over and over: "*Please* can I get out the science stuff? Can I? Can I? Can I?" "Can't I wear a T-shirt and shorts just this *one* time?"

Lights Out

When the day is done and you're all worn out from playing and learning, it's time to go to bed. Sometimes it's hard to take a bath and brush your teeth and wind down for sleep, but be sure to keep using your obeying manners even when you're tired. You might be rewarded with an adventurous story, a gentle back rub, or some extra bedtime songs.

Good night! Sleep tight!

Food—yum!

No matter where you are or what you are eating, you can use your best table manners to make mealtimes happy and fun for everyone.

Mealtimes are when we fill our bodies with food and our hearts with fun and laughter. You can tell your parents all about your morning at preschool. You can make up silly stories with your brothers and sisters. You can ask your parents a million questions about everything—from cars to stars.

Table Setting 101

Mealtime manners start with a little dose of helping manners—setting the table. It's fun to set the table, and you can start learning how to do it! Just ask your mom or dad to teach you how, and you're on your way.

Getting Ready

Go into the bathroom and wash your hands thoroughly. You can sing "Happy Birthday" while you wash your hands—even if it's not your birthday—so you know that you've washed your hands long enough to get them nice and clean. Then go to the table and sit down with everyone else.

Many families say a blessing—a prayer to give thanks for the food—and every family has its own way of doing this. You can hold hands, take turns saying the blessing, or even sing your blessing!

Time to Eat!

When you're ready to eat, pick up your napkin and put it in your lap. If you're eating something really messy like spaghetti or tomato soup and you have on nice clothes, you can also wear a bib.

Sit still in your chair and sit up straight with your elbows at your side (not on the table). Never rock back and forth in your chair or climb on the table. That could cause big spills—for the food *and* for you!

Table Talk

It's fun to talk at the table, but make sure you chew your food first and swallow it, *then* talk. Just pretend that your mouth is a door that automatically closes when you're chewing food.

Eat and drink quietly—no loud chomps or wild slurps. Take small bites and little sips. Use your utensils, not your fingers, to eat your food (unless you see your parents eating certain foods with their fingers).

Families have different rules about playing with your food. Some parents let their kids make spaghetti roads and graham cracker skyscrapers. Some don't. If you're at someone else's house or if you have guests over for a meal, it's best not to play with your food.

Finishing Up

When you're done eating, you can nicely ask, "May I please be excused?"

Before you go play, help clear off your dishes, wipe up any crumbs or spills at your place, and carefully push in your chair.

Then say a great big "thank you" to the person who made the meal: "Thanks, Dad! Those pancakes were the best!" "Thanks, Mom! I love your chocolate pudding...and I love you!"

My Partytime Manners

MAKING THE MOST OF FUN TIMES

Parties are great! You get to play games. You get to give—or receive—presents. You get to eat lots of yummy food and have an awesome time.

Big Parties, Small Parties

Sometimes it's fun to have a small party with just a few good friends. You watch a movie, eat big slices of pizza, play some games in the yard. Other times you might have a big birthday party or a gathering for your whole team or Sunday school group.

You and your parents can send out the party invitations to everyone on your guest list. Pretty soon you'll find out who will be coming, and then very soon it will be time for the party to begin. All right!

A Great Gift-Getter

Be sure to say out loud who the gift is from, read any card (and you can pass the card around), and then open the present. Hold it up for everyone to see and then say a great big "thank you" and something nice about the present: "Cool soccer ball!" "Great book!" "Wow! Look at all of these Legos!"

It's My Party

When your friends come over to your house for a party, meet them at the door and make sure everyone knows everyone else. If your friends bring presents for you, say a big "thank you" and put the gifts aside until present-opening time.

Your mom or dad can help you explain what you're going to do and what you're going to play at the party. And even though it's your party, you should never act bossy or tell everyone what to do.

You can set a good example for the games by doing a good job of taking turns and by letting the youngest person at the party—maybe your little brother or sister—go first. (Sometimes, if it's your birthday, you get to go first!) Be happy for the kids who win games. Better yet, before the party you can help your parents plan some games where everyone wins!

Thanks for Coming!

When it's time for the party to end, go to the door with each of your guests as they leave. Thank them for coming and thank them again for any gifts they brought.

Being a Partygoer

The next-best thing to having your own party is going to someone else's party. You'll want to dress up at least a little bit if it's a birthday party. If it's a swim party or a party at a play place, wear what would be best for that.

When you get to the party, first say hello or "happy birthday" to the guest of honor. Then you can give him or her your gift and say hello to anyone else you know. It's also very good manners to say hello to anyone you don't know. You might just meet a good friend that way!

Join in the Fun

Go along with what everyone else is doing. Some parties have a lot of planned games and activities. Other parties just have a lot of free playtime. Either way, just join in the fun! If you don't know the rules of a game or you're unsure what you are supposed to be doing, just ask a grown-up.

Sometimes it's hard to watch one kid open present after present when there's nothing for you. But remember that when your birthday comes, you will have lots of gifts, too! And there are lots of gifts for guests at parties—the food, the decorations, the games, the favors.

When it's time to leave the party, find your host and his or her parents and then thank them: "Thanks so much! I really had a nice time! Happy birthday!"

My Growing-Up
Manners

Every day you're learning new things—how to play sports and games, how to build new things, maybe even how to read and write!

As you grow up, you keep learning new manners. And they're easy to learn if you just remember the Golden Rule: Do unto others as you would have them do unto you.

Let's Talk About It

Way back at the beginning of this book, you learned how to talk to new people and how to use polite words. It's always important to be friendly to people and to speak clearly, but it's also important to be safe. It's probably not the best idea to walk up to a bigger kid or a grown-up you don't know and start talking to him or her. It's a better idea to get one of your parents to come with you and to talk to the person together.

Oops!

And even though you try your best to use good manners and to do the right thing, sometimes things go wrong. You make a joke that hurts your friend's feelings. You accidentally break your sister's toy. You leave a mess for another person in your family to pick up. What should you do then?

The best thing to do is to say a great big "I'm sorry" that you really, really mean. And then you can do something to make it better. Along with a grown-up or older sibling, bake some cookies for your friend whose feelings were hurt. Ask your parents to help you fix your sister's toy that was broken. Do some extra chores around the house to make up for the mess you forgot to clean up. Soon enough, all will be forgiven and forgotten.

In any situation, just remember to be kind and considerate of others, and your good manners will follow right along. You're off to a terrific start!